How to Succeed
as a
First-Time Manager

Dr. Terry Carter

ISBN 979-8-88540-983-4 (paperback)
ISBN 979-8-88540-984-1 (digital)

Copyright © 2022 by Dr. Terry Carter

All rights reserved. No part of this publication may be reproduced, distributed, or transmitted in any form or by any means, including photocopying, recording, or other electronic or mechanical methods without the prior written permission of the publisher. For permission requests, solicit the publisher via the address below.

Christian Faith Publishing
832 Park Avenue
Meadville, PA 16335
www.christianfaithpublishing.com

Printed in the United States of America

To my mother who believed in me even
when I did not believe in myself.
To my dad who sees beauty and loves all my
siblings and me unconditionally.
To my sweetheart who loves me and encourages
me every day to be my best.
To my wonderful team of Angels in Scrubs who
give me a reason to be grateful daily.
To my brothers and sisters who remind me of my roots.
To all my peers who show me what is possible.
To all my bosses who teach and mentor me
every time I interact with them.

CONTENTS

Acknowledgments vii
Introduction ix

Section 1:   Managing You, the Manager 1
Chapter 1:   The Five Reasons Before You Say Yes 3
             Action points for chapter 1 12
Chapter 2:   I Have the Five Whys—Now What! 13
             Action points for chapter 2 20
Chapter 3:   How to Detach from Your Previous Peer
             Group (PPG) 21
             Action points for chapter 3 27
Chapter 4:   Decide and Choose Your Peers/Friends 28
             Action points for chapter 4 34
Chapter 5:   Separation from Your Title 35
             Action points for chapter 5 39
Chapter 6:   Have Your Values and Principles 40
             Action points for chapter 6 44
Chapter 7:   Pledge Not to Please Everyone 45
             Action points for chapter 7 48
Chapter 8:   How to Believe in Yourself and Love Yourself 49
             Action points for chapter 8 53

Section 2: Managing the Business 55
Chapter 9: Business and Budget Lingo 57
 Action points for the business and budget lingo 62
Chapter 10: The Meeting Lingo 63
 Action points for the meeting lingo 66
Chapter 11: The Dress Code Lingo 67
 Action points for the dress code lingo 69
Chapter 12: Email/Text Message Etiquette 70
 Action points for emails/text messages etiquette 73
Chapter 13: Managing Your Time 74
 Action points for time management 79
Chapter 14: Job Requirements/Expectations 80
 Action points for job requirements and
 certifications 82
Final Word 83
Appendix A 85
Appendix B 86
Appendix C 87
Appendix D 88
Bibliography 91

ACKNOWLEDGMENTS

To Linda and the Christian Faith Publishing who made this book possible.

INTRODUCTION

> People will forget what you said, People will forget what you did. People will never forget how you made them feel.
>
> —Maya Angelou

This book is meant for managers who are either transitioning to the manager role or are in the manager role for only three years or less. The book can also benefit the informal leaders who are thinking of pursuing a career in management or leadership. While this book relates mainly to the health care industry, the book will benefit any manager or leader who has two or more direct reports.

My promotion to first-time manager was over ten years ago. Despite having been an expert in my field of study, having excellent technical skills, having had practiced in more than one continent, having gone to graduate school, and having read enough books on management and leadership, nothing could have prepared me for my new role.

On Wednesday, October 19, I was a staff employee, and on Thursday, October 20, I was a manager. To be honest, I was on cloud nine, and I had all these ideas in my mind on how to serve the team, lead the team, change things in my department, and to a certain extent, change the world.

Unbeknown to me, my life was about to change. At 11:30 a.m. on Thursday (the first lunch as a manager), I walked into the break room as I had always done over the years with lunch at hand. I was hungry and ready to eat. The staff members who I knew so well as they were my friends were in the break room, eating and chitchatting. As I settled into the only empty chair, my former colleagues in the room stopped talking and eating. The room became awkwardly quiet. They all stood up, and one by one they all walked out of the break room. In less than two minutes, all the chairs were empty, except the chair I was sitting on. The room was silent, and I was the only one in the room. There was no mistaking what had taken place—a walkout. I was not prepared for this walkout action. I suddenly felt alone but not lonely and wanted to speak or say something. My immediate thought was to open the door and stop them from leaving. My second thought was that I needed to leave my lunch and follow them (after all, they were my peers and friends); but then again, I was hungry, and I needed to eat. My heart was filled with some emptiness; although to save face, I tried to act courageous with the hope that someone else would come back to the breakroom. It was in this duality of states—heart emptiness and mind courage—that I started to eat. As I ate, I decided to put my brain to work and tried to figure out what the walkout meant. In a split second, my ego kicked in, and I thought, *You know what, this was no big deal, after all, I was single and eating alone, or being alone was not new to me.* For heaven's sake, I lived alone. I did most of my stuff alone—shopping, driving, etc. The only time I got together with my friends was at work, in school, or during some special occasions, like birthdays. For two minutes, as my ego continued to bid me to speak to make me feel better, I "inhaled" my food like only a hungry wolf would. As I slowly silenced my ego and filled my hungry stomach with some much-needed nutrition, reality hit; I was now a manager, and if I could not even influence my team to share a meal with me, how was I going to influence them to help me tackle the many outcomes I was now faced with. I finished my meal and headed back to my new office and got busy thinking, planning, and praying.

I searched on the website for books on transitions, books on the first year of management and leadership, and I sure could not find one that fit my experience.

This book is a labor of love; it is the book I wish I had especially on that first day when I felt empty, yet I had to save face and act courageously. This is the book I would have picked up for days when nobody showed up on my door to congratulate me or celebrate my major achievements. This is the book I would have picked up on those days when I needed someone to at least acknowledge that no one has all the answers and that management/leadership is a never-ending journey with no destination other than personal fulfillment. This is the book I would have picked up when I needed someone to get me back to focus on what is truly important to me—succeed in my leadership journey and have fun succeeding.

Use this book to save yourself many years of searching and avoid many avoidable mistakes. Most importantly, use this book to propel yourself to what is truly important to you during your first three years and beyond in your manager/leader journey.

Go have fun leading!

SECTION 1

Managing You, the Manager

CHAPTER 1

The Five Reasons Before You Say Yes

The first time I said yes it felt great; the second time I felt wonderful; the third time I had some doubts; the fourth time I wondered what I was thinking, but the fifth time I was so sure that nobody was going to stop me, not even my dear mother.

—Dr. Terry Carter

When the time has come when you feel the itch that you want to be a first-time manager, that's great! To "scratch" the itch, do yourself a big favor and ask yourself at least five questions as to why you want to take the new role of becoming a manager. Until you have more than five reasons to your five questions written—yes, written down—answers as to why you want to be a manager, then do not even try or at least step back before scratching that itch. I am begging you, please do not skip this process, as this first process will save you time in the long run before you cross that bridge of well-deserved promotion. In addition to saving your time, this process will save you enough heartache, pain, and grief, so please bear with me.

One or two reasons will not be enough to keep you engaged or inspired to become a manager; for when the going gets tough—and I promise you, the going will get tough and tougher—you will need more than two reasons to continue and move forward. A word of caution: The time to find your reasons is not the time you get the offer but the time you first think of becoming a manager. Do not panic, though, if you are just thinking about your reasons right after the offer as you still have some time to get this done as it's better late than never. Sit down, get your pen and paper, and get busy thinking and writing. You are setting yourself up for success by going through this first step. You can do this!

The consequences of not identifying your reasons are too great to take the risk. Some of my friends who I love ended up losing their first manager job within months because they wanted "to try to see if this was for them." Others wanted to be managers because they were comparing themselves with their current manager (I can do better than my current boss). Worse still, I have a friend who has worked in three hospitals in less than four years as a manager even though she still does not really know why she wants to be a manager. This emotional attachment to the idea of becoming a manager with no definite reasons as to why has led to her losing those three jobs in three different organizations while she still believes nevertheless that she is supposed to be a manager. She does not really know why because she has not taken the time to examine how her values of meaning can be aligned with and added to organizational objectives.

The process of identifying your reasons is made easier by using comparisons and contrasts. For instance, compare your strengths and weaknesses to those of a manager or leader you admire. You can do this easily by reading the works of your current or past leaders. If your current boss inspires and influences you, check and find out what exactly your manager does or has that you are attracted to. Is it the communication style? Is it their knowledge? Or is it their time management skills or team management skills? Then see how you can grow your strengths by using those of your hero leader. Align your strengths with what you admire. Word of caution: Work on being your authentic self and not a copycat of your hero.

A second method that works is by first learning from someone what the role is and drawing from the role the things you learn to do and those that you have a natural inclination to. For instance, if a manager role requires you to coach and supervise more than one direct report, and you have no desire to coach or to learn to coach individuals, then don't even try to be a manager even if someone volunteers you for the role. The action of self-reflection relies on you knowing and understanding yourself. After you are sure that the role will be a good fit for you, then craft an image or a vision of what you want from your new role in thirty days, three months and three years. Once you identify what you want, you might get your reasons as you are seeking the new role.

If after soul searching, you cannot come out with at least five compelling reasons as to why this position is for you, then you can give yourself some peace of mind and stay where you are.

The next move as you cross that bridge of reframing your identity is to have five or more answers to those five initial whys and to find out the reasons why the person who made the offer to promote you did so. In simple English, this means why the boss promoted you or selected you to become a manager. In most cases, this individual is usually the person you report to directly or the person in charge of the department or the unit you will be promoted to and working in. Have a meeting with them, and ask them to share with you their five reasons or more about why they made the decision to extend the offer to you. The way you phrase that question to get your five reasons is up to you, but a word of caution, here is to not be tempted to glibly say, "I want to know why me and not the ten or so candidates who interviewed with me."

By getting and writing down your answers and reasons to those initial whys and then adding the top five reasons from your boss, you are now on your way to having most of the tools you will need in your success toolbox and be on the lookout for those strengths that your new boss sees in you that you may not be completely aware of but which have already been mentioned by her.

How so? Well, in my case, when I completed a strength inventory review, I remembered that my boss mentioned the fact that I was very positive in my interactions, a trait I had never given myself much credit for. Once you have had that meeting, and hopefully you have more than five reasons from your boss, celebrate this great achievement toward your new journey.

After the celebration, plan some time, sit down, and seriously do a comparison between your several reasons and your boss's reasons for compatible match/matches. Capture the matches. And if there are some conflicts, find out how to resolve the conflicts in a beneficial way to you. This process requires you to tell yourself the hard truth and do a great reconciliation of those reasons. You will have a great start if you come out with a minimum of five compatible reasons. Place the compatible reasons in your new manager tool kit. Keep in mind that the higher the level of conflict between your reasons and your boss's reasons for your promotion to manager, the greater the likelihood that you will not be successful in your new role. Likewise, the higher the number of matches, the likelihood that your transition and growth in your role will be successful.

Just imagine your boss has tasked you with and is expecting you to go north, and you are headed east while both of you are trying to end up at the same place and destination, which in this case is north. There is no way this will be possible for the obvious reason you are both headed in different directions. You will both end up at two different destinations, two different productivity outcomes, so to speak. Your boss expects you to run parallel, and not perpendicular, to you and your goals as you will be both working on implementing specific program goals and objectives within a broader organizational matrix of mandates. If or when you reach what I call a juncture of unreconcilable reasons, and you find out there is no way to reconcile the reasons, remember, your boss is not going to change for you. That means, if your boss is headed north, and you are stuck heading east, your boss is not going to go east for you; instead, your boss will look for someone else who can go north with, not you. My task and intervention for you is to have a good conversation with yourself and look at why those maps of meaning and productivity outcomes varied. Face the reality of those whys as this is the time, an opportunity, for you to decide to either *step up or step down*. I consider this reconciliation as the first decision point in your career as a manager, first intervention having crossed that bridge of reframing your identity.

The second step after reconciliation comes in when you decide to *step up*. Allow me to say that congratulations are in order as you have enough reasons and hopefully enough drive to move you forward. At this point, believe it or not, you are more prepared than half of your cohort.

What's next, you ask?

Your contribution.

This is a time where I will ask you to really dig even deeper and ask yourself what it is that you are bringing to the table—that is, what are your contributions to the team, your boss, and your organization. Find a big reason as to why the team, your boss, and the organization should invest in you as their new manager. At this point in your journey, it's not the time to look at yourself and answer arrogantly, "Why not me?" Rationalize not and lie not to yourself. Put your ego aside for the moment, get out of your head, and think not only about what is unique to your skill set, but also what you can share with more than two people. In other words, what do you really want to contribute with your new team members in meeting the overall productivity goals? And how are you going to serve the team and your organization? Drawing from previous work experiences about a challenge facing the team or your specific organization makes for a good start. Some folks, though, may be tempted to glibly say, " I know enough to share" or "I do not know much" without first counting the cost of contribution.

Yet, I invite you to intentionally dig deeper, in the spirit of Myers-Briggs, as every life experience brings with it so much to share with love, joy, fun and intuitive knowledge in meeting the cost of organizational contribution. I remember in my case when I started. I had expertise in clinical, technical skills. And though I was unsure about my unmapped identity as a manager, I did know one thing: I love food, travel, and fun. And so when I got promoted, I almost busted my financial budget because I wanted to share with my team all the different types of foods, places, and fun I had experienced. In hindsight, this is the people-skills strength that my boss saw in me but did not recognize so easily in myself. In addition to loving food, traveling, and having a penchant for fun, I gained experience in hierarchical politics by coming to know many people, learned how different departments worked, and became familiar with what other leaders viewed as their "north." This strength has taught me that if I'm not having much fun at what I'm doing at work, then I'm not doing something right.

I urge you to look for three things or more that are unique to you, and you can share with your new team. One of my friends loves to hold parties, and so she can throw a party at any time to celebrate an achievement.

If you are being promoted within the organization, take an inventory of the things you know that new people joining to the organization don't know, things that you take for granted, such as knowing the parking spot, the right elevator, the buildings, or other people.

These are a few of my well-traveled maps as manager that tasked me with organizational intelligence compared to new leaders joining the organization. Maps of reconciliation and stepping up are tools that I invite you to consider in your new role as manager as well!

Why you? The third order of business will be to ask yourself the following question: "Why you and nobody else?" Please answer this question seriously. Do not be tempted to say it is because you have a bachelor's degree, a graduate degree, or own a Maserati. People in the workplace do not care what you have earned or own; they mainly need to know who you are as a human being and how you can relate to them as humans with love and compassion. They are looking for someone who can serve and guide them through their daily struggles or needs. They also want to know that you can work with them for them. People want someone they can be comfortable relating to, especially regarding their secrets and things that matter most to them. They are looking for someone who can empathize with them. The more authentic you are, the better. No one wants to relate to a robot even when they are paying their telephone bills.

People want to be seen, heard, and cared for—not necessarily in that order.

The next thing to ask is why this is important to the people you want to serve. If for any reason you have no interest in serving people, then you have no business seeking the position as a manager or leader. To be honest, if the first thought that closes your mind when you hear a phone ring or beep is a curse, please stay away from your new offer. I am begging you to either say no to the promotion offer or start a new relationship with your ringing phone as part of your tool kit. If not, I can promise you, that the promotion will only help you increase the frequency and intensity of the uncouth words coming out of your mouth every time your phone rings or beeps.

The team that you are preparing to lead needs someone who can answer their questions either on the phone; in person; or by email, text, etc. The team needs a coach, a leader, and most importantly, somebody who does not see them as problems or an annoyance, aka an inconvenience. You have two options or opportunities at this stage in your new role: see your phone as a tool/resource to help you as you serve and as a powerful tool to influence your team strategically.

The final order of business is to set your goals high for this managerial role and experience. Set your goals for the next three months, three years, and thirty years. You can easily do this by asking how success will look for you in those next three months, three years, and yes, thirty years. Set and know your achievements in the form of written goals and know the metrics and the pathways you will need to measure your success as the science of self-improvement demonstrates. This level of ongoing self-analysis can be challenging, but in my SKIP, 3 Cs and Action Points found at the end of each chapter, I have distilled for the reader maps of meaning to enable you to do just that as you apply them to each year's challenges of contribution. These three motivational and team building strategies will help you adapt and develop managerial habits that are practical and contribute to your evolving productivity landscapes. Annual revision based on new insights you've gained will allow you to sustain successful bridges to your thirty-year plan".

After identifying your success goals, visualize and plan your celebrations in advance as you see yourself succeeding. Get into the celebration details by planning for your outfit, the location, the guest list, and the success speech you will give. When I did this part of my journey, I was full of joy. I selected my party outfit. I imagined myself in Tuscany, Italy, in three months. (I was promoted in October, so three months got me to the holidays, including New Year.) My bubbly toast speech theme was "Success in Leadership Bash," and I saw myself celebrating with a bottle of Italian champagne, Prosecco. I literally saved the money for the bash. And during the times when the going got tough, I created a countdown to my celebration and worked a little bit better and smarter. The three months went by fast. And while I was not in Italy that New Year's Eve, I was invited to my boss's house because I celebrated New Year's Eve with not only my boss but also with my team and their friends. I looked wonderful wearing my new outfit to the party. And even though I did not make the bubbly speech, I had a great time. The celebration party was such a success and so real, a moment for me that when I went home at 2:00 a.m., I started writing my three years' "bubbly toasting speech."

The master planner. When you are working on the reasons why, you are the *master planner*, and you are the creator of your masterpiece manager life. For the master planner role, you have already acquired a few vocabulary tools in your toolbox, which are as follows: why, reconciliation, step up, visualize, service, expand goals.

This is how you *SKIP* to your masterpiece manager life and the three Cs:

*S*ee yourself as the manager you are ready to become and tell yourself the truth from your mind, heart, and soul. The temptation to want to think about what others may think of you as the manager may seem helpful, but at this point, the best thing to do is to follow your own truth. Make sure that the masterpiece manager role is what you want and is what you were created to do. Notions of "try" and "failure" are not an option.

*K*eep a mind's eye upon those classical transcendentals of the good, the truth, and the beautiful. Enjoy the simple moments as you work through what you want, and plan your life to be.

*I*ncrease your focus to what is your heart's desire and passion.

*P*atience as you navigate your new role is important as sometimes you will be faced with situations you have never even thought existed.

The three Cs:

*C*ontain your emotions, especially the emotions that do not serve well—e.g., the emotions of anger and/or fear. Find the emotions that are destructive to you, and replace them with emotions that are constructive. Realize that you have the power to choose what you want in your life. You do not have to offshore your life to anybody else, so you owe it to yourself to create a masterpiece. In my many years as a manager, the worst manager I experienced was a manager who was leading from a place of anger and existential angst.

*C*aptivate your imagination, and create enormous dreams for this managerial role and beyond. Create a big vision of your life, not only as a manager but also your life as a living human being.

*C*ontrol what you can, especially the great habits of laughing, listening, and working hard. Let go of what you cannot control, especially other people and the weather.

Action points for chapter 1

Reasons why you want to become a manager:
Write down the main reasons you want to become a manager and why you *must* become a manager.

1. _____
2. _____
3. _____
4. _____
5. _____
6. _____
7. _____
8. _____
9. _____
10. _____
11. _____
12. _____
13. _____
14. _____

CHAPTER 2

I Have the Five Whys—Now What!

Love yourself first and everything else falls in line. You really have to love yourself to get anything done in this world.

—Lucille Ball

Great job if you are still with me this far. You have made up your mind that this promotion is for you. This is the moment you have been waiting for, so let's get going. To be honest, you are among the few who get promoted and succeed versus the many who fail in the role within the first three months.

The sole survivor. This phase of your new role deserves a new identity for you, so congratulations are in order as you have acquired a new name, "sole survivor." You will feel like you are alone at this phase because you are just about to lose your previous peer group (PPG), and now you have a boss who just literary spits out all the expectations for the quarter or the rest of the year. I was promoted in the fourth quarter, so this resonates with me. At this point, professionally speaking, you will feel like you are by yourself. And you better believe it; you are. Regardless of how alone you feel, the reality is that you are not really alone. This period lasts for three to six months. Some people spin in and out of this phase over the whole six-month period, while others get out of this phase as fast as a month or two.

The best relationship to have as a *sole survivor* is relationship with yourself. You will experience a sense of loss. And your former friends, while they cheered you on your promotion, will also have mixed feelings, which range from loss, excitement, to jealousy. Yes, the same friends who cheered you on will be asking you how you are doing. And if you happen to tell them you are really enjoying your new role, you might notice that they do not have any more words to share. This reaction of lack of enthusiasm for your job enjoyment might come like a shock to you as you might start wondering as to whether your PPG/friends did not want you to succeed. The reactions are totally normal. Give your PPG some grace as the fact is they are also going through a period of loss and confusion as they do not know how to behave in your presence or you as their new manager. As you will notice later, and probably to your surprise, your friends are busy figuring out their own lives to care about your transition. Just put yourself in their shoes, and realize that now your relationship with them has changed for the better as you need their support as you work on not only serving them but achieving your productivity goals. Give them and yourself some grace, and treasure previous moments as you plan on creating new memories together. Second, face the truth that you cannot continue hanging out with your PPG if you want to be successful and move forward.

The sole survivor tool kit. The first tool in your toolbox as a sole survivor is a pair of sharp scissors—yes, this is not a typo. You need a pair of scissors to help you with the first order of business, which is to separate yourself from your PPG, especially if they are now your direct reports. Yes, you must cut the cord and learn to be comfortable with yourself. Love them, and wave them bye for now. They will be back in your life, not as your peers but as your team, and you as their leader. This separation will feel weird as you will have a void. But instead of feeling empty, work at filling the space with love for yourself and them. I mean, be your best friend and love yourself so much more than anybody else ever can or will love you. This will feel weird for the first time. And if you are either stressed or confused, you may start reaching for your comfort food, ice cream, or chocolate. It's okay to reach out for your comfort foods, but for heaven's sake, do not be tempted to go back to your PPG. Cut the cord and mean it. This process takes guts and courage. Personally, I had no clue, and my PPG made it easier for me by leaving me alone in the break room—a reminder that I had taken more than enough time to cut the cord. I thank my team every day for this gesture as they made my cutting the cord easier. In addition, the team let me know that they will hold me accountable if I did not shape up fast and show up as a leader. The cutting of the cord should ideally only take seconds or minutes in our mind's eye, but be patient. You can be honest with the PPG to the point you feel comfortable, but let them know you are busy learning your new role, which you are.

The best way to spend time with yourself is to have moments of silence and solitude, and listen to your mind's heart and soul as you work on yourself. In silence, you will be able to take a major inventory of not only your mind's strengths and weaknesses but also an inventory of your heart's desires and your soul's passions.

The second tool for the sole survivor is a mirror—yes, a big mirror where you look yourself in the eye anytime you need to tell yourself the truth, even when the truth hurts. There are a multitude of truths that you should be telling yourself at this time to ensure your successful transition to your new managerial role. One truth should be that you do not know everything there is to know about being a manager. The realization that you will have to reach out to others who have been there is worth the price of your mirror. A second truth is the fact that you are one partly ignorant of the managerial role and are prone to blind ignorance, at times, as you think you know what needs to be done. In addition to all the truths in the world, the mirror also serves as a tool to stop and appreciate yourself even when you mess up. Yes, sometimes you will mess up even with great intentions. Whatever else you want your mirror to represent is up to you, but for heaven's sake, the mirror should not be a reason to criticize your love handles or your new acne pimples on your face. I have a mirror in my office, and the mirror serves three purposes: (a) I make sure I look presentable to the team. (Yes, I make sure I do not mess my beautiful smile up with spinach on my teeth.) (b) It affirms to me how beautiful, loved, and enough I am as I look myself straight in my face and eyes. (c) It reminds me to be grateful as I have eyes to see myself, my goals, and all the beauty around me.

Whatever your reasons are for looking yourself in the mirror, write them down, and use your mirror.

The third part of our tool kit is a great book. Whatever you like reading is your choice. But as a new manager, a start with leadership classics is not only a necessity but a must. When I was in graduate school, one of the professors recommended the book *The Seven Habits of the Most Successful People* by the late Stephen Covey. Thank God, my professor did recommend this book, as this was the first book in my toolbox. As a manager, you will need to build your own mental attitude and brain muscle to prepare yourself for both the simple and the tough challenges ahead, and there is no greater way than reading a great book daily. Reading also helps to build your mental capacity and capability. Believe it or not, reading from the greats will not only give you the tools on how to deal with the same challenges the greatest men and women deal or have dealt with but will stimulate your creativity and imagination. The other reason cultivating daily reading as a great habit is that it will help you to adapt to dreaming big dreams again as well as help you work on your own personal and professional goals by igniting your subconscious, imagination, and intuition. Lastly, I believe you do not want to be the most illiterate manager out there, as Stephen Covey notes with no apologies, "The person who does not read is no better off than the person who can't read."

In addition to reading, dare to dream big. To help your dreams, think of one that involves what you would really like to do and of places you would like to see and why. Think about the beautiful things you want to do in your lifetime. The day-to-day life of a manager or leader is not an easy one. There are always planned and unplanned scenarios that present themselves, and you must learn how to deal with these scenarios. Better yet there are scenarios that you can never learn from anybody, but you must experience yourself and figure out what to do at that moment. One such scenario was when I was in my first year of manager. I had one of my direct report's significant other show up to work after a breakup. The employee was so scared, and she went into hiding for her safety. I had to face the irate significant other, deescalate the situation while at the same time saving my employee's dignity. And though one can take a course in dealing with irate individuals, no course prepares you to connect with the heart and soul of individuals, particularly in this situation and to the extent you're able to help them deescalate their angry emotions followed by their giving you a hug as they learn and grow from such an unforeseen experience. A great way to capture an individual's attention is to look at the good and great in everyone, including yourself. Look for one positive, great word you can describe any individual you encounter, and treat them with the lens of that word, if nothing else. Some words to start with are beautiful, fantastic, lovely, etc. This one word will help you to shift your attention and your energy.

The fourth tool in your toolbox is your favorite snack—yes, your snack. Whatever your favorite snack happens to be, have it, and buy more as the more the merrier. Saving an extra snack is a great idea as there may be times you will need to share, and it allows you to be distracted from the tasks at hand for a moment and reset your imagination. Besides, you never know who might come knocking on your door one day, and sharing your snack may also help you learn something new, or an updated procedure needed to save someone's life. The favorite part about this tool is supposed to be fun and to remind you that you are still a human being, and you will need to not only eat sometime, but you deserve to enjoy those little pleasures in life. I am a firm believer in a life well-lived, and I am so convinced that there is no living if you cannot enjoy whatever brings your soul some joy. If your favorite snack is a piece of candy, by all means, have the piece of candy and enjoy. My snacks collection changes with my pleasure goals and what I am in the mood of enjoying. I celebrate even the smallest forward footsteps.

The fifth tool in your toolbox as a sole survivor is a box of Kleenex®. Like it or not, you will cry in your new role. Sometimes you will cry for joy, and other times you will cry for other reasons other than joy. When the crying moments happen, you will need to close your door, finish your crying business, clean up, look yourself straight in your eyes as you stand in front of your new mirror, and then get out there and serve. Yes, remember you are in charge. And unless you know how to lead yourself, there is no way you are going to lead others. Yes, if it hurts, it's okay to cry. Even if your parents told you that men don't cry, go ahead cry.

Your tool kit is almost complete, and believe it or not, you are now more prepared than half your newly promoted cohorts. You are working your way to overseeing, solving a multitude of problems and solutions, and you are a little bit more prepared to complete more tasks than you were before. In addition to the five tools, you want to learn how to think, not only on your feet but also on the go.

The sixth tool you will need is a ton of patience. Yes, patience will get you through the times you feel like you know everything (sometimes more than your boss), but the truth is you do not know as much as you think you might in this new role. Patience will also be necessary when you are not only dealing with everybody else but also when you are dealing with yourself. Give yourself time to learn and grow. Remember, you need to take care of yourself to take care of others in your team. No one likes an impatient leader even when they are in a line, renewing their driver's license at the public department of transportation.

Last, but not least, wrap all these tools with the gift of belief in yourself. You can do this! Know that you are not only the player, coach, and manager, but you are also your new cheerleader. Honestly, the hard reality is that no one—and I mean nobody—is going to be knocking on your door each day or every moment to cheer you up, inspire you to be your best, and to remain motivated. Make it your first order of business to not only motivate yourself but also to enjoy things that keep you motivated, energized, and inspired. You deserve it, and you are worth it!

Congratulations, new manager!

You have cut the cord. You have loved yourself by telling yourself the whole truth. You have read the greats. You have enjoyed your favorite snack. You have cried. And most importantly, you have a new belief in yourself that says, "I am going to do this, and all is going to be all right." So what is next?

To be empowered and to help you summarize the relationship with yourself, remember and use SKIP and the three Cs.

*S*earch your soul, and seek out those classical transcendentals of the good, the truth, and the beautiful. Your soul will guide you out of even the darkest nights.

*I*nclude your reasoning as a necessity of course, but be able to shut your mind, at will, as you search and seek out your soul's creative imagination. Together, reason embracing creativity. Treat your mind as you would treat your best friend with temperance, knowing when to invite them in and when it's time for them to go in your mind's eye.

*K*indle and treasure with gratitude every moment that is worth your pleasure.

*P*ractice in a place of gratitude and magnificence. Realize that there are no limits in what you can and will accomplish. The only limits are those you place on yourself. So if you got to dream, you might as well dream big. "Whether you think you can, or you think you can't, you are right." Henry Ford.

The three Cs:

*C*oncentrate and focus on what it is that you are preparing or prepared to do.

*C*aptivate your imagination, and see what is possible in your new role and beyond your role.

*C*elebrate every achievement, regardless of how minuscule you feel the situation is.

Great, now you have the tools in your toolbox, and you are well prepared and empowered, so go out and become the best manager!

Action points for chapter 2

Write down a list of three books you will start to read.

1. _____

2. _____

3. _____

Write down which sole survivor tools you are committing to use and why.

1. _____

2. _____

3. _____

CHAPTER 3

How to Detach from Your Previous Peer Group (PPG)

"It's Hard to Soar with the Eagles when You
Have to Live with the Turkeys".

—John C. Maxwell

You got your scissors, and you have cut the cord, and you are feeling a sense of loss. This feeling is real. Identify and appreciate the feeling as you are a human being; and with a thankful heart and mind, continue to move on. Whether you like it or not, you will have to detach from your PPG if you want to succeed in your new role. You must cut the cord; otherwise, you might as well kiss your promotion goodbye. For those who failed in cutting the cord, they are no longer managers. This is the reality. Your team is looking for a manager and not a friend. Remember my story about my former peers leaving me alone in the break room? This was a reminder that my detachment had taken more than twelve hours while it should have taken minutes. I am so glad my PPG made it easier for me by literary kicking me out!

Hopefully, your PPG kicked you out as well and made it fast for you, but if they did not stop you, then fret not as I will guide you through the process.

The tenacious tiger. In the sole-survivor self, in addition to having a pair of scissors, it helps to look at yourself as a tenacious tiger—a corporate metaphor to be sure—on top of the tallest tree in the wilderness, lying on top of the strongest branch. Imagine this feline stretched out, mapping its territory and laying the strategies for both survival and success. Imagine you are that tiger on top of your world, stretched with greatness, and you have mapped out your territory and are going to succeed no matter what. Now know that you got what it takes, and no one, not even your best friend or your mother, can stop you. Now invite others to your new managerial world as you dare to become unstoppable!

First order of business is to plan for a meeting with members of your PPG and thank them for their vote as their manager. Also, thank them for being in your life. They will appreciate you more if you let them know the fact that while you love their company, your new role now has placed some limits on what you can share with them as well as how much time you can spend together. As much as you can share, ask them for their support, and let them know that you are still struggling to learn the ins and outs of your new role, and you believe this process will take much of your time. If you used to hang out with them, especially during your days off, let them know that you will not be available to spend as much time with them as you did due to your new role. They will understand, and most importantly, they will appreciate your sincerity.

In addition to meeting with your team, you will need to be grateful for your team. Yes, "your ability to see beauty and possibility is proportionate to the level which you embrace gratitude," as Maya Angelou revealed. Yes, gratitude is a must if you must lead your team. Keep in mind that you are detaching yourself so that you will be able to embrace your new role. And with that, there is a level of finesse that is required. I can't tell you how many times I must remind myself to be tactful even at times when I feel like choking someone for supposedly something they did that I happened not to like or approve of.

After meeting with your team, plan on what you are prepared to achieve as a manager. The first person who will give you a sketch or a template of your plan is your boss. The first or second meeting with your boss should be very important to you as this is where you will learn what is expected of you and what the time lines are, so tune in fully and ask questions if some things are unclear. Most of the organizations work by quarters. So depending on the timing of your promotion, find out what is the priority item for the quarter and for the year. Find out what the measuring metrics are especially if you are new to the organization. Some bosses are very straightforward, and they will guide you through the details, while others will give you the resources to help you figure the details out. There is no right or wrong way; what matters is that you have a clear understanding of your role expectations and are conscientiously mapping out your new metaphoric territory.

Once you know what is expected of you, it is up to you to figure out how you can make this happen fast and meet the deadlines. Ask questions, and verify what is not clear. There should be no gray areas in interpreting the outcomes you are charged with. In addition, please do not assume anything. Figure out how well you want to communicate your own needs. Honestly, your boss is human and not a mind reader. I once made a mistake of assuming that my boss would approve payroll on a Monday since I was off duty. My boss called me while I was out on vacation to confirm what time I was planning on having the payroll approved. I honestly had not planned on approving payroll when on vacation, but I did not communicate effectively with my boss on the fact that I would be needing help approving payroll while I was on vacation. So communicate effectively; do not assume that your boss will take on your responsibilities when you are out on vacation. Your boss has her own responsibilities to carry; so plan, communicate, and verify. And please do not assume.

Second, find out from your boss what resources are available for you to learn and assimilate to your new role. Make use of the resources, and effectively communicate your plans. Nothing is upsetting to your boss than having you in class when the boss expects you to be coaching a staff member or working on a budget item for the next day's meeting.

To sum up, the tool kit for the tenacious tiger are gratitude, communication skills, and resources for your growth.

To make it easy to detach from your PPG and to figure out your new role, you can *SKIP* to your magnificent self and the Cs by doing the following:

*S*earch for the best talent that will fit with the PPG. After all, you were once a member of the PPG, so you should be able to find the best matches for the team. Look for the talents that will complement your team to become a better team. If you did not like your PPG, and you would like to change them up, that is okay too; however, you will need to manage everybody effectively, either in the team or out of the team. In addition, search for the resources that you will need for your personal growth, especially on communication skills, and use those resources diligently.

*K*eep the best talent and the culture of the PPG. Manage those who need to be managed out of the culture with minimal interruption to the team. Remember, you have the team working with you for you, so the greatest gift you have right now is the team. Invest time to assess, and reassess the team periodically, perhaps monthly as the needs change. *K*eep yourself informed and at pace with your expectations, and fulfill what you commit to do.

*I*ndulge your team by engaging them and challenging them to think differently. Care about them, and treat them as individuals, not just as members of your team. Encourage them to care about each other as well. Be optimistic, and provide autonomy for the team. *I*ndulge yourself with new ideas that serve you well as you transition into your new role with greater productivity by continuing to read and adding new motivational speakers to listen to, like John C. Maxwell, Tony Robbins, Zig Ziglar, and Jim Rohn, each month diligently.

*P*raise your team and the individuals in the team for what is going well, and praise their strengths. Speak positively about your team, and manage/utilize them through their strengths. Look for the good in others each day by choice, and maximize the goodness. *P*raise yourself, and pat your back when you do something you are proud of. Do not wait for anybody else to praise you. Seize the power of now.

The three Cs to use for the team are geared toward celebrate, congratulate, and coach.

*C*elebrate your team by celebrating whatever they may be celebrating individually. I remember one time in the recent past when in the middle of a meeting, one team member shouted, "My son passed the bar!" She was on cloud nine. Instead of shutting her down or reprimanding her for interrupting the meeting, we all cheered and celebrated the moment with her. To many, this may seem like mixing personal and professional lives, but this is real life.

*C*ongratulate the team members for whatever is worth congratulating them for. I can give lots of examples, but another event which I remember is when one of the team members passed her certification exam. And as she whispered to me, I literary stopped what I was doing and called for a small party to celebrate her achievement. It took less than twenty minutes, but to this day, she is my best motivator for those seeking certification.

*C*oach. Remember, life does not stop because you are the new manager of the team. Life still goes on, and your team will need continuous coaching, especially when you have competing priorities regarding your new role. Done right, coaching is what is going to save you much frustration and agony, so plan out enough time to coach a minimum of two people a day. This could be on-spot coaching or planned/scheduled ten to fifteen minutes of coaching.

As you navigate your new role, there are times you will be tempted to go back and be with your PPG, but the rule here is to save yourself first to be able to help others. It's kind of like the adage of the airplane where you put your oxygen mask on first. The longer it takes for you to detach, the harder it will be for your success moving forward. At this point, most people are tempted to worry about your PPG. But believe me, do not waste your time worrying about everybody else, so to speak, as everybody else, including your friends in the PPG, are busy trying to see how they will fit in your world as their new manager in pursuit of their own career goals. Your role is to *step up* as the honeymoon period is short, and no one remembers it anyway except you.

In summary, to detach from your PPG, you must make use of *SKIP*: *S*earch for the best talent, *k*eep the best, *i*ndulge, and *p*raise the best *as* you and the three Cs *c*elebrate, *c*ongratulate, and *c*oach.

Action points for chapter 3

Write down three goals your boss wants accomplished this quarter.

1. _____

2. _____

3. _____

Write down three goals your boss wants accomplished this year.

1. _____

2. _____

3. _____

Write down three things you want to communicate with your boss.

1. _____

2. _____

3. _____

CHAPTER 4

Decide and Choose Your Peers/Friends

> We herd sheep, we drive cattle, we lead people.
> Lead me, follow me or get out of my way.
>
> —George S. Patton

You have grown in self-confidence and have practiced diplomatic, patience-testing leadership skills. You have detached yourself from your PPG, and now it is time to push forward and continue enjoying your new role. At this juncture, I am going to introduce you to the next order of business, which is to select a new set of peers—your new peer group (NPG).

Caution: If you did not separate yourself from the PPG, and you skipped the sole survivor part, please go back right now and complete that section as you do not have the tools to move forward. If you successfully graduated from the sole-survivor role, kindly disregard the first sentence and know that you are now ready to either join an existing group of your peers or create one if there is none in existence.

The great collaborator. In this role, you have a new name, "the great collaborator," and you have two tasks.

This part is going to be easy as you have only two main things to do, either you choose to join an already formed peer group which you like, or you choose to create one.

HOW TO SUCCEED AS A FIRST-TIME MANAGER

First and foremost, you must figure out why a peer group is important. You see, as a manager, you are like the inside of a sandwich between your team and your boss. Yes, the fact is you are sandwiched between your team and your boss, and you must learn to make the best use of that fact. Both your boss and your team need you to manage them successfully and get everything else done. What this means is that you cannot show up to either cry or be out of control. At the point where you feel you need to have a conversation, running things through the peer group comes in handy. The peer group becomes your outlet to learn new ideas and sometimes become a venting arena. You don't want to vent to your boss. And worse still, you do not want to vent to your team. Before you laugh at the idea of venting, think of yourself at your maximum frustration, and you must vent, or something is just going to give. Now in that state, think of yourself facing your boss and venting. I don't think you have to imagine further what will surely happen. My guess is that you do not want to imagine the consequences that will follow. That's why your NPG becomes your best friend. The NPG team will also get you out of your misery by helping you double-check your email when the stakes and emotions are high before you hit send and commit career suicide. Imagine, you just had a meeting or read an email you did not agree with the content therein, and you are back at your desk and typing as fast as your keyboard can type. Since you are fired up to respond and give the sender "a piece of your mind" or "your side of story," at this point, you may want to call a member of your NPG and run your email draft through them. If a member of your NPG tells you to sleep over the draft before you hit send, please listen to them. If they tell you to send the email to yourself if you must hit send (yes, that happened to me), then agree with them and send the email to yourself. You can then revisit the issue the next day or at a time when your emotions and stakes are not as high. But besides the obvious, why is the peer group important? Wait a minute, this does not mean that your NPG is where you go to complain and/or whine necessarily, but this is your new team where you run those ideas that are either easy or complicated or both. Other benefits of having NPG include, but not limited to, creating long-lasting professional friendships/relationships and "growing up" in management and leadership together.

Now that you know the benefits of NPG, the next step is how to find or create your NPG. The first rule is to make this process fun and not very complicated. Start from where you are, and reach out to a minimum of two or three other managers. The easiest way to do this is to go one-floor level up or down and find out who the manager or managers are. If you are not in a metropolitan area with big multilevel buildings, do a horizontal department search, knowing that you will surely find other managers in your organization.

If you work in a small organization with no managers or are the first manager, then you are in for a great time as you are going to create an NPG with other managers outside your organization. This is also the case if you are a business owner, and you are the only manager. We will get to the creation part of NPG shortly. In the meantime, if you are in an organization with multiple managers, and you have identified those to reach out to, it is best to reach out to the managers physically and not via email or text because this part will require not only your mind to navigate, but it will also require your heart. Your heart speaks volumes when in the presence of strangers and helps you determine who would be a match for your "friend zone." The next reason you want to be meet in person is because you can assess very keenly if the manager you are dealing with is an integrator or a segmenter. Once you find each manager, ask them two questions: Is there a formal manager group they're already a member of? And how many members are in the group?

The answers to these two questions will help you determine if there is an existing manager group or not. If there is an existing group, find out when the next meeting will be held and the name of the person to contact to get an invite. If no manager group exists, ask if they would like to be in one which you will be leading. Yes, if there is no peer group available, you will create one, and you will be the leader. So brace yourself as you are about to create the best group of friends. This will be a great step to work on your interprofessional skills.

Usually, a peer group of three is the best as it is easy to manage when you are new since it's easier to learn about two people as compared to learning about ten or more people.

Your role as the leader of the NPG is that of a great collaborator since you will be helping in coordinating the new members of your NPG.

The great collaborator tool kit. The tool kit for great collaborator role adds on to your sole survivor tool kit and is as follows:

You need a notebook to write down your meeting details. Start by finding out what is the most challenging need the NPG is facing and how they would like to tackle as a team. On the notebook, work out details of how they would like to meet (in person or virtually), how often they would like to meet, and how long should the meeting be when they meet. Should the meetings be formal or informal? And do you meet over a meal or a cup of coffee/tea? Do all the members have to meet at a designated time? Or do you meet two at a time, if more than two? Do you call and schedule meetings? Or can you just show up in each other's offices when problems arise? What happens after you meet? Are there ground rules, like sometimes I just want you to listen to me vent without interruptions and no feedback *or* sometimes I want the honest feedback? What do you discuss? Or can you just have the other person listen as you speak without advice and/or opinion? How many people are in the group and how do you invite or recruit new members? The smaller the NPG, the easier it is to manage, especially if this is your first ever group meeting or are coordinating a group of more than three, which may become an added burden for you.

The next tool, in addition to a journal and a notebook, is a working phone with a great camera to take pictures and capture the moments. In addition, these smartphones serve as tools to remind you that you need to keep in touch with your NPG.

The last tool in the toolbox is a journal. You will need a journal to write every one of your achievements at the end of each day as you capture the great ideas and takeaways each day presents to you.

Just a reminder about meetings, it is very important to keep in mind having a clear, keep-it-simple agenda for each meeting even if the agenda is venting all the frustrations for the week as the members involved need to be prepared and know what to expect. You do not want to be faced with a need to manage disruptions created by lack of direction. Always remember, friends at work are important, and you want them engaging with you until they become distracting. So set the ground rules early. The purpose of the NPG is for collaboration and not a distraction or, as they say in the United States of America, not to be a "pest."

The agenda also needs to include time to celebrate the wins. Set and lock down times to celebrate, whether it be weekly, monthly, or biweekly. Look for reasons to celebrate, whether work-related celebrations or personal things, like birthdays.

When I got promoted, there was no formal manager group, so I helped create one with three new managers. I am so glad I did, as over the years, I have come to appreciate the benefits of an NPG in addition to creating long-lasting relationships and friendships.

SKIP to your NPG with your dream team, and excel to new heights of your evolving manager self with great anticipation.

*S*earch for your new peers in your work entity or outside your organization.

*K*eep your NPG in the *k*now, especially with current issues in each organization they may have missed.

*I*ntroduce yourself and others to the benefits of NPG, and have fun as you may lead the NPG.

*P*repare in advance to avoid wasting time by getting off track.

The three Cs:

*C*reate or join an existing NPG. Learn the benefits of an NPG, and produce a great dream team of your peers that you are proud of. You have no limits as to who you can put in your NPG except, of course, the fact that they cannot be members of your PPG, as we have covered. Make a list of the things you envision your NPG accomplishing, be enthusiastic about it, and go out there and deliver with no apologies. You can do it!

*C*ontribute and make NPG worthwhile. Everyone wants a giver and not a taker. The most important key in the NPG is you have got to contribute. In the NPG, if you do not contribute anything of value, you will be eliminated so fast before you can even say your name. Remember, the NPG is a team of peers. And while venting is helpful, it must not be abused as you must always add value to others, as John C. Maxwell admonishes.

*C*elebrate the wins together. Remember to celebrate the wins of your NPG—simple things like birthdays, marriages, the birth of child, or the achievement of outcomes. Find out what your group members are excited about, and genuinely celebrate with them. The NPG is a team of peers who also need your support, not only in celebrating achievements. Remember that because challenges in life may not always lead to a celebration, also be prepared always to console your NPG members if the situation calls for consolation to help them navigate through what John Maxwell highlights as "failing forward," choosing, on purpose, to turn any failure into an asset.

Things are going great. You have an NPG, and you are now creating relationships with a team of your peers whom you are collaborating with, contributing to, and coordinating events with, as well as celebrating the wins. And so what's next?

I know some of you reading this may wish to ask how they will survive their new managerial job with an NPG that may only have two members. This is actually all right as we remember that the NPG is a fluid, ever-evolving, and growing team of your friends who are your confidantes and with whom you are now able to share your experiences at work. Your NPG will attract those of like mind just by networking, having the goal of resolving practical challenges, much like study groups found aplenty on any university campus. Again, and to that end, developing the NPG will involve you reaching out to other departments managers and physicians, aka folks who are already helping you run your department. Think about your department, and see who else may be helping your team accomplish their goal. You'll likely find a diversity matrix of interdepartmental networks. This could be the supply chain department, the housekeeping department, the human resources department, etc. Each of these groups are necessary for you to accomplish your job. The NPG is not a requirement for your job but a strategy to make your job a lot easier and help you succeed. Most importantly, the NPG is a group of your friends whom you can trust and enjoy the leadership journey. So choose wisely. Most importantly, the NPG will be your support so you do not go venting to your boss and/or your team.

Action points for chapter 4

Write down three people you will recruit or reach out to as your NPG.

1. _____
2. _____
3. _____

State three benefits you wish to gain from you NPG.

1. _____
2. _____
3. _____

Write down three ways you plan to involve your NPG.

1. _____
2. _____
3. _____

CHAPTER 5

Separation from Your Title

> The best day of your life is the one on which you decide your life is your own. No apologies or excuses. No one to lean on, rely on, or blame. The gift is yours—it is an amazing journey, and you alone are responsible for the quality of it. This is the day your life really begins.
>
> —Bob Moawad

Congratulations, you stepped up. You have successfully separated yourself from your PPG, and you are now in your NPG and have a tool kit that supports your managerial career goals. The next order of business is to learn to separate yourself from your title. Yes, you are reading right. You have worked hard to become promoted. You now have a title as a manager, and you have the keys to an office. Things are going very well, and now you must separate yourself from your title. I promise, this must happen because you need to introduce yourself by your name first and not by your title. Your title should come to play only if you are signing your name when somebody else is introducing you. Another exception is if the situation calls for it, especially if you are asked. Do not be so caught up in your title to the point that you do not recognize your own name. You are you first, and your managerial title supports your role in the team, so get clear and separate the two. Your team also needs to learn the same. And when they see you, they should be very comfortable by addressing you by your name and not your tittle. Introducing yourself as "I am the manager" is not only annoying but downright tacky. I have been fortunate to serve so many people, living and some on their deathbed, and none have come to me and said, "I am Manager or CEO Jane Smith." They all, every single one, have introduced themselves by name and not by their title. Honestly, the only people who seem to like to be addressed by their title include past and present presidents of nations, heads of states, the royal family, and, yes, of course, physicians and university professors found in our medical research institutions. Though we are making exceptions for these, just simply drop the title and be yourself.

It takes a good deal of authenticity for people to see you and address you by your first name. For instance, my organization's CEO is known by her first name. I am so proud that my team and my colleagues all, every single one, introduce me by my first name. Most people, including my customers, do not know me by my title. They know me by my name and nothing else, which bears particularly fruitful results with my monthly metric outcomes for customer service. As I previously noted, the only people who enjoy being introduced by their titles are past and present presidents of many world nations, heads of states, and the royal family. Since we are none of these, enjoy and celebrate your own authenticity of service and add value to our customers. There is joy with names and meaning. If you do not believe me, try calling one of your friends or direct reports the wrong name, and they will be sure to correct you on the spot. Worse still, try misspelling their name and see what happens. Better yet, have someone come to you and call you by someone else's name and see how you will react.

You should be proud of who you are as an individual, regardless of your title.

Make no mistake of identifying your self-worth with your title or your job.

Yes, you are now the manager, but remember, you are still a human being with needs; you still walk the same hallways everyone else, including your team, walks on. God forbid, if something happens to you, especially health-wise, a team member will be the first to come to your rescue and possibly start compressions or call a code blue or 911 for help. The reality of life is that you are serving the team. And while you may have the title, the team is there working with you for you. In addition to sharing the hallways, you share the same roads and the same community, so treat people with respect, and treat people like the human beings they are with their own daily challenges. Be kind to yourself and to others. "Kindness is wisdom," as Philip J. Bailey frames it so well.

Always remember that life does not stop for you when you get promoted to becoming a manager. In fact, life now expects more from you, and you have got to show up and make a difference, not only in your own life but also in others' lives. As the Good Book says, to those much is given, much is expected.

I am grateful I had no problem with separating myself from my title as I learned this lesson long time ago from my algebra teacher who let the whole class know that he was Dave. If we made a mistake of addressing him as an algebra teacher or Mr. Dave or sir, he would correct you on the spot, and he would get your attention to where you never repeated the mistake again. I liked his style. And when I grew up and was in the workforce, I decided to adopt his style. To this day, I love the fact that people, including my direct reports, call me by my name and not by title.

And while we're discussing names, please avoid the habit of creating nicknames for people.

Tool kit for your separation journey. The tool kits to add to your toolbox for separating yourself from your title are authenticity and kindness.

Let people know who you are by your autobiography of a life well lived and not by your title.

SKIP to your own authenticity by taking charge of your life, and make a point to love and respect your name.

Search for great mentors—alive and those who have lived an autobiographical life. You can do this by engaging your life with reading great autobiographies of great leaders. When you have a wonderful living mentor, remember to be a prodigy and not a parasite by adding value to their life as well.

*K*ey in on your heroes and your great memories. Develop a habit of looking up to your heroes in leadership when faced with challenges and wonder what they would do, then do it!

*I*mprove your knowledge daily, either by interacting with your heroes, watching, or reading the greats or by putting yourself in proximity with those who inspire you to become a better you, like John C. Maxwell, Zig Ziglar, Jim Rohn, Stephen Covey, or Peter Sage.

*P*ractice gratitude daily, and get real. This life is not a rehearsal as you practice today and live tomorrow; it is the reality. So get real, and enjoy living as yourself and not as a job-title imposter.

The three Cs:

*C*onserve your time for the things you love and enjoy.

*C*ovenant with and savor new knowledge.

*C*elebrate the crescendo when you get to your goal or meet your hero.

Action points for chapter 5

State your three main reasons for separating yourself from your title.

1. _____

2. _____

3. _____

Identify three people in leadership who do not use their titles.

1. _____

2. _____

3. _____

Write down three things you will do moving forward to be more authentic.

1. _____

2. _____

3. _____

CHAPTER 6

Have Your Values and Principles

> Values govern peoples' behavior, but Principles govern the consequences of those behaviors. Principles are independent of us. They operate regardless of our awareness of them, acceptance of them, liking them, belief in them or obeying of them.
>
> —Stephen Covey

As a manager, you will need to take some time to rethink or rewrite your values and principles. If at this point you have not created a blueprint of your values/principles, this is the best time to start and finish. The reason this step is important is because you will need "you, yourself, and you" to solve some real challenges that will come your way. Be a creator of what you want to happen in your life. As you write your values/principles, ignite your creative subconscious genius and keep feeding your passions in life as you keep in mind the fact that nobody wants to be led by anybody who is not themselves led by values and principles, such as those already mentioned in chapter 1, recalling those classical transcendentals phenomenologically embraced by a diversity of cultures throughout our shared history. You must first lead your own life with a proven track record by those first-order principles before you have the privilege to lead others.

Your major job as you write your values is to dig deeper in your heart and soul as to what you are committed to as you. My favorite Sunday school song goes something like "not my brother, not my sister, but it's me, O Lord, standing in need of prayer." When I became a manager, I changed that Sunday school song to "not my boss, not my team, but it's me, o Lord, standing, in need of guidance." Mostly, I remember that song when I must dig deeper in my heart and soul. You may choose a song or a phrase for yourself. In addition, depending on the leadership literature specific for your values and principles, which may help, keep in mind that a majority of the books written on management mostly focus on management skills, like how to successfully manage cash flow, systems, marketing/sales, human resources, and other related areas but usually not on how to manage and lead yourself. Self-management is one of the most important skills to master, so do yourself a big favor and make it easy for yourself and all those you will have the privilege to lead and manage by managing thyself first.

The master creator. In that spirit, we'll be strategically adapting new role names or personae in the pages to follow. We'll begin with that of a *master creator* specific to tooling managerial skill sets. For our purposes, I'll draw from an admixture of Jungian self-analysis with Napoleon Hill's self-improvement psychology. Currently, you are creating both new and evolving personal values and principles specific to your new position. This step is made of serious and complex decision-making, sometimes subconsciously as mentioned. So if you want to be successful, you should take time and put your best foot forward with earnest commitment.

Think of things that you want to do, and commit to them. Think of your personal philosophy to life and living, and create your life around what you stand for with untiring zeal. Sometimes, when going through this exercise, it helps to think about those traditions that you grew up with. I remember my parents saying something like, "In this family, we treat everyone with respect and as a person of value." Though, unfortunately, not all families inculcate respect and value into their children as the sociological literature evidence, I had the great benefit of such and easily adapted these skills into my personal "bag" of values. It's here that adopting those transcendentals have served me well. And knowing that these may be cultivated by all who have an earnest interest in personal self-development regardless of background makes "values govern behavior" realistic for all of us.

Tool kit for the master creator. For the master creator's task, you will need the following tools:

Soul Searching—you will need to think about your own personal philosophy regarding life, managing people, as well as managing your life's many personal challenges.

The second tool in your toolbox is *honesty*. You must be truthful. Remember, this is your life and no one else's, what your life is all about, what things you can do, and what things that you will never do under any circumstances.

The third tool in your toolbox is *time*. Yes, you will need some time each day to sit down and think. Some people take thirty minutes a day, while others take an hour or more. The amount of time is optional, but you will need to do it consistently, daily.

Lastly, you will need your journal or your notebook to write down all your values/principles in the spirit of Zig Ziglar's deliberative admonition of the necessity of writing down personal development goals. Remember the business adage: If you do not document it, it never happened and is not done. Therefore, writing down your values and principles is a great way to ignite your subconscious as you go back and review them, particularly during those most challenging of times which will come and as you listen to yourself when discussing them with your NPG.

All right, master creator of self-analysis, you are well on your way to becoming a person of magnificent values, so SKIP to your magnificent values/principles by doing the following:

*S*earch for what you stand for. "If a man hasn't discovered something that he will die for, he isn't fit to live" (Martin Luther King Jr.).

*K*indness goes a long way to both yourself and even strangers.

*I*ncise what you are no longer going to accept moving forward.

*P*ay it forward following your heart. Look out for someone you can touch or help daily.

The three Cs.
*C*ontrol your vision; it is yours and not everybody else's.
*C*arry out your vision, mission, and your principles.
*C*elebrate even the small wins.

Action points for chapter 6

Write down three values/principles that you remember since your childhood.

1. _____
2. _____
3. _____

Write down three values/principles that you can never live without.

1. _____
2. _____
3. _____

State three things you love about your values/principles.

1. _____
2. _____
3. _____

CHAPTER 7

Pledge Not to Please Everyone

"The purpose of life is not to be happy. It's to be authentic".

—Peter Sage

To be successful in your role, you must make a pledge to yourself to avoid trying to please everyone. Remember to keep this one pledge, as in reality, you will not be able to please everybody with your actions. Some people will not like you for being you, so save yourself the trouble by making and keeping a pledge to not be a people pleaser. It is no secret that if you are pleasing everyone, you are doing what I call KB (kissing butts). Successful managers are not in any way in the business of KB, but they manage everybody, including their bosses, especially in public. See people as they are, and meet them where they are without being a KB. If you cannot make this pledge right now, then please do yourself a big favor and acknowledge this habit in that mirror we previously discussed and pledge to change as folks can smell a "KB agent" a mile or two away."

There is no secret that you cannot be everything to everyone. Be the one person who will show up every day as your authentic self. The truth is that people do not care that much about you as they are busy caring about themselves and their own agendas and less about you. When they show up at your door, they are mainly looking at what you must help them with to succeed with their agendas. And if you are being a KB, you are making it very easy for them to manipulate you to their advantage. The message is having a backbone and stop being everything to everyone right now.

In this role, your new name is a *role model*.

The tool kit for a role model. The tools you need to succeed as a role model will help you to stop or to not be a KB.

The first tool in your role model tool kit is a backbone. You have one, so use it with confidence.

The second tool in your role model took kit is the word *no*. Yes, you can say no to your direct reports, your boss, and even the company president and get away with it.

The third tool in your role model tool kit is a vision board to use and create your own future. You have your life to live, so start living your life by having great visions of what you want your life to look like, both as a manager and as a human being. Create your masterpiece life, and live your life to the fullest. Done right, you will realize you do not have time to be a people pleaser as you are busy living and creating your masterpiece life, having already begun drinking in the many insights of Napoleon Hill.

SKIP out of the habit of KB, and live your masterpiece life with the three Cs.

*S*earch for people you admire, and learn from them. Once you have wise counsel, use it and pay it forward by helping someone else.

*K*ick the habit of KB to the curb, and forget it forever. Nobody wants a KB, even if they do not tell you to your face. You have more to offer your team and the world than spending your time as an expert in KB.

*I*nclude someone in your circle of new NPG friends to hold you accountable for good behaviors (i.e., the behaviors you want to adapt instead of being a KB).

*P*ledge to kick the habit of being a KB and mean it. Take only a few minutes recognizing if you have a KB problem, and move on after this awareness. Let the ones who are supporting and encouraging you as a KB know you are no longer a KB by your changed habits, and pay it forward consciously.

The three Cs:

Courage—Have the courage to tell yourself the truth and kick the KB habit. In addition, have the courage to look at those who used to be a KB to you, and let them know you have moved on. You can also show them by your new approach and deliberative habits.

Care—Care much about your future self, and stop being an imposter. Think about your life in three years and in thirty years as you do not want to be known as the manager who was an expert KB. You must change for your future self, if for nothing else. Remember, your masterpiece life is waiting for you, so don't waste any more time.

Catch yourself when tempted to be a KB again, and *c*hange immediately.

Action points for chapter 7

Write down three things you will start to do to create your masterpiece life.

1. _____
2. _____
3. _____

Write down three things you are committed to doing to be a great role model.

1. _____
2. _____
3. _____

Write down three things that you are proud of.

1. _____
2. _____
3. _____

CHAPTER 8

How to Believe in Yourself and Love Yourself

> "Many intelligent adults are restrained in thoughts, actions, and results. They never move further than the boundaries of their self-imposed limitations".
>
> —John C. Maxwell

Lastly, perhaps the most important advice for this first section is to believe in yourself and love yourself. Everybody will, at one point, give up on you, and like it or not, the reality of life is as D. Kelly eloquently said that there are only three who care about you: God, yourself, and sometimes your mother. You owe it to yourself, at the bare minimum, to know that you are enough, and everything that you need is within you as you change your workplace beliefs. In simple English, this means that you have what it takes to not only lead your team to success but succeed in your new role.

Tell yourself the truth, including those things you are uncomfortable with as needed. The one thing to avoid is telling the truth by exclusion. Lay it all down in front of you: the good, the truth, and the beautiful. The truth will hurt sometimes. And the joy is that when it hurts, it will only hurt once since you will have the courage to address the issue and either accept things as they are or change those things that are hurting. In contrast, if you exclude the truth, you will be hurt repeatedly many times, too many. Save yourself the heartache of telling yourself lies, and change course to the truth.

Your name, as you believe in yourself, is the *loving soul.*

It may seem a little out of place to be writing about love and belief in ourselves in a self-improvement book, but changing work behaviors begin with our psychology, followed by corresponding behaviors acted out. As the title of James Allen's pamphlet suggests, "As a Man Thinketh, So He Is." And so yes, I am broaching this sometimes-unspoken mindscape as its relevance is easily found within cognitive-behavioral therapy literature.

The tool kit for the loving soul.

The first tool for the loving soul tool kit is a good book or a magazine that makes you happy.

The second tool in the loving soul tool kit is a recipe for your favorite dish.

The third tool in the loving soul tool kit is a name of your favorite restaurant.

The fourth tool in the loving soul tool kit are the gadgets for your favorite hobby.

Once when I told one of my new managers to "love thyself," she looked at me like I had three heads! She just could not fathom the idea of loving oneself. You see, daily she had turned out to be a very task-oriented manager to a point where she would forget her orientation about who she was or where she was at times.

This manager reminded me of my own journey when I started out as a manager; it was all about me. God knows that in addition to my big ego, I had so many flaws and insecurities, which made me show up as such an uncaring person on the unit. I was so results-oriented. And it did not matter how I got the results, but I needed those daily productivity results. I forgot to let myself and the team be who we were as people, and soon we all became unproductive as far as the performance metrics were concerned. This egocentric behavior led me to so much heartache to where I literary forgot how to laugh and have fun as I worked. It was not until I spoke with my mother one day who noticed that every time I talked to her, I was only talking about those things I either accomplished or were planning to accomplish. My mother, who I love, stopped me in my tracks and asked one simple question, "Child, when did you decide to become a human doer instead of a human being?" I was caught off guard. And to be honest, I did not have an answer. I asked her what she meant. She explained to me something I will never forget: that my conversations with her were mainly about achievements or the next goal in life, and she was really becoming concerned. After that conversation, I did reevaluate my life, and I made changes not only on my schedule but also on my passions in life. I noticed that I had not taken a vacation in two years. One of my passions is traveling across the globe. So after that conversation and self-reflection, I got busy choosing my next vacation time and destination. Thank God I did as the vacation I took back then changed my life journey as I met one of my mentors in life who has guided me through this new journey of growth. In addition, I started being more ethnocentric conscious as opposed to being egocentric. That vacation, followed by returning to work and resuming life responsibilities afterward, also helped me to become more centered and focused on the realization that I'm enough, and everything I need is within me now, existentially, by faith as I have the privilege to interact and serve a diversity of peoples within my health care setting, forever changed by evolving COVID-19 challenges.

Taking about two or three minutes to appreciate simple privileges of the senses, we sometimes take for granted things like breathing, seeing, feeling, smelling, or even walking, does the human soul and heart so much good. Appreciating these simple privileges is a good start for those who find themselves being stingily results oriented again while getting stuck in believing in themselves takes a back seat.

SKIP to your own enjoyment with the three Cs.

*S*eek the counsel and guidance of those you love and those who love you back. This could be a great friend, a mentor, or your parents, the ones who love you so much that they will tell you the truth, even when the truth hurts. Think of those people who love you and those you love.

*K*eep the good habits and great beliefs about self, and ditch the ones that do not serve you well.

*I*ntegrate great habits and beliefs with your passions and your heart's desires.

*P*ass on the practice to those you love. Remember, there is a lot to live for, and the best way to live is to enjoy living.

The three Cs.

*C*hange course based on great counsel and if the occasion calls for a change. Have an awareness of the necessity of change and reevaluate your intentions after an intervention.

*C*ongratulate yourself by the end of an hour or the day for simple things like stopping and taking a good, deep breath. Enjoy the power of the senses, and be grateful.

*C*elebrate small wins daily, even if nobody else except you is noticing your wins. You owe it to yourself to celebrate your achievements.

Action points for chapter 8

Write down three books or magazines you will read for leisure.

1. _____

2. _____

3. _____

Write down three names of people you love and people who love you.

1. _____

2. _____

3. _____

Write down three of your favorite recipes.

1. _____

2. _____

3. _____

SECTION 2

Managing the Business

CHAPTER 9

Business and Budget Lingo

"The chief business of the American People is the business".

—President Calvin Coolidge

If you are still with me, you are one of the special, wonderful human beings who I can call the ultimately successful manager versus those who will struggle to win the manager game. Give yourself a big hug, and know that you are not alone. I am with you in spirit.

Take some time to celebrate your major achievements. Let me help you as I sum up as you have done great so far.

You have done the following:

- Detached yourself from your PPG
- Decided to create or join an NPG
- Separated yourself from your title
- Reidentified your values/principles to live by
- Stopped pleasing everybody
- Believed in yourself and loved yourself

You are all set and ready to rock your new managerial role to successful heights. By now, you are almost nearing your ninety days into the role. So if not already done, we can stop here and celebrate your thirty- and sixty-days wins. And for the three-month wins, you can start to write your "bubbly" speech for those challenging three months, and get busy planning for that great milestone. You are doing great, and the world of management better watch out as you are an unstoppable human being and manager!

And now, we will change gears to the business side of the managerial role.

You are now a manager, and this is new territory for you as you were promoted due to your technical skills. Take some time to learn a few things about your new role. Some of these may look like common knowledge, what I call the spoken language of the business. While some though looking, like common knowledge, is the unspoken language of business.

The business lingo. First and foremost, learn the new business lingo. Regardless of the industry you are in, there is the operations side of the business and the technical side of the business. In the health care industry, there are the clinical and the operations parts of the health care business. To help clarify the two sections, the clinical or technical part of the business is where you are seeing the clients/customers, while the operations part is where you are looking at how many people you will need to take care of the clients/customers, amongst other things, like the environment, the inventory, the costs, the bills, etc. Depending on whether you got promoted from the clinical/technical or operations part of the business, as a manager, you will need to learn and develop a working knowledge in both areas. For instance, if your background is clinical/technical, you will need to learn the operations part of the business and vice versa.

I was mainly clinical, so I had to learn the operations part of my hospital's business. The operations learning included, but was not limited to, knowing my full-time employees and the full-time equivalent (FTE).

For this section, I will go through the business lingo in four different sections, namely the budget lingo, the meeting lingo, the dress code lingo, and the team speaking lingo.

The budget lingo. For the budget lingo, your new persona name is the *solutions specialist.*

The budget lingo encompasses many operation facets, from staffing to the facilities. You must learn fast how to calculate the number of employees you need to run your department efficiently and the metrics used to calculate the number of employees. The calculating part is not as hard as people would want you to believe. But what is important, and nobody tells you this, is how to perfect your budget lingo to communicate effectively. I can give many examples of the budget lingo from my first budget meeting, but let me focus on the first scenario that comes to my mind.

Your boss asks you what your variance is, and you are feeling quite excited, and your answer sounds or looks something like this: "I am very short as I need five new employees. I can't seem to balance the schedule, especially with the call ins and two employees being out on vacation. It is getting to be quite difficult, and everyone is working so hard." You just earned yourself a big F for failure on your budget lingo transcript. You may be surprised and wondering why you got such a low grade since, to you, the answer sounds logical, and after all, you are doing great regurgitating the facts, which you have on your spreadsheet. No doubt, these are the facts since you are quite short on your staffing schedule, and you are doing everything possible to cover your "holes" in the schedule, while everyone in your team, including you, is working so hard. To answer your question, I would like to compare your response to the following reply, which is the correct manager's budget lingo, and probably your boss's expectation: "I have a 3.6 FTE variance, and that is a split between all the shifts, so I am able to cover the variance with some overtime (OT). Looking at my numbers, I am still within my productivity margins even with the OT. I am actively recruiting despite the fact that the recruiting pool is not as full as it used to be. I have reached out to the team to refer their friends as I continue to work closely with the recruiting department to see how we can work together to backfill the positions and reduce the variance further." I guess I do not have to tell you which of the examples written show of a manager who knows how to use the budget lingo effectively.

I know you might be tempted to say that you are new and just starting out, so you will learn, and you are right. That's why I am with you here to guide you so you do not make the same mistakes I made during my transition. I was the one who responded in the way I described in the first example, and I was also the same person who, three years later, gave the reply outlined in the second example. Had I known then what I had learned three years later, I would have saved myself some heartache.

To be clear, the initial example is a regurgitation of the numbers and an expression of the problems, which any boss you are reporting to will already have and know through generating their own metric reports. The second example represents a matrix combination of the problems and what you are doing to solve what are daily routine issues.

When it comes to the budget, you will need two tools in your *solutions specialist's* tool kit.

The tool kit for the solutions specialist.

The first tool you need is *problems* to solve. The problems may be in terms of resources, usually in the form of adequate staffing or capital.

The second tool is a *budget expert (a real person and not recorded material)*. The easiest way to learn the budget lingo is to spend time with the head of your organization's operations department and/or NPG. You will need to find out who this person is. And when you identify them, you must do whatever it takes to meet with them and, if possible, invite them for lunch or coffee. Whatever you do, it is up to you. But try to meet with them and introduce yourself and let them know you are new to the role. It is all right to say in this meeting that you have no clue, and you are willing to do what it takes to learn, and then do it.

Be prepared with questions as to what the numbers mean, how the numbers relate to your role as a manager, and what you need to do to learn as fast as possible. Once you are clear with the numbers, then you must practice solving the problems you are facing with tangible solutions. This meeting is meant to expose you to the expert and the resources available in your organization. If you are a business owner and you are solo, then your task is to reach out to an expert accountant in your area of business and do the same thing. Invite them for lunch and/or coffee and pick their brains, so to speak.

As a solutions specialist, you will need to learn to look at problems from the solutions' point of view. And when you approach your boss, especially, part of the business lingo involves stating the problem and then spending more time explaining the many or few ways you have either worked or are working to resolve the problem(s). Once you become so versed with the business lingo, you will find yourself stating the resources you need from your boss as well.

In addition to reaching out to the experts and practicing your business lingo, you will need to research some books on finance. You can easily find these books as some of them are part of graduate programs.

SKIP into the Budget meeting with the Cs.

*S*tudy and understand your numbers, especially before a budget meeting. Reach out to folks, especially those with a finance major, mainly those folks working in the finance department of your organization or the experts in your field of work.

*K*nowledge about your budget is vital to everything you do and your overall success. Seek out relevant information regarding your industry and your department, avoiding the temptation of getting too caught up in the complexity of the numbers.

*I*nvest some time, and know the numbers. You can do this, either formally or informally, by immersion with business-oriented books, especially finance books, etc.

*P*artner and collaborate with others who are helping you get the job done. It is important to understand how your business operates and connect with those people who are helping, either your department or your organization, accomplish the mission and goals of the organization.

The three Cs:

*C*arom and learn the business lingo to help you communicate effectively as a manager.

*C*anvass your organization for the financial gurus, and join them in their meetings if possible.

*C*atalog the "must-know" to run, and manage your unit's business with financial integrity, and leave the rest to the CPAs.

Action points for the business and budget lingo

List three budget problems you are to manage.

1. _____

2. _____

3. _____

List three people who will help you with your budget problems.

1. _____

2. _____

3. _____

Write thee actions you will take to solve your budget problems.

1. _____

2. _____

3. _____

CHAPTER 10

The Meeting Lingo

"There are two keys that determine who we are: who
we conceive ourselves to be and who we associate".

—Anonymous

As a manager, you will be required to attend unit meetings, either in person or virtually. It is very important to understand the meeting etiquette before you end up embarrassing yourself in front of your peers or your superiors. I know you probably have attended a meeting and wondered when someone would stop talking, as the more they spoke, the more pitiful they sounded, and the more you felt sorry for them, leading you to wonder when they would catch themselves and stop the embarrassing scene. I have attended quite a few. And in Texas, you know the person has reached the point of total embarrassment, and the gig is up when you hear people say, "Bless his or her heart."

To avoid embarrassing yourself and having people "bless your heart," the first thing you want to know is who invited you to the meeting and why. Second, figure out if the meeting is a group meeting or a one-on-one meeting. Third, find out if the meeting is in person or virtual. If virtual, ask if your camera is supposed to be turned on or off. The exception for camera being off is for interviews, especially with first-time interviewees, when observing affect is crucial.

If the invitation did not include an agenda or your role in the agenda, reach out to the meeting organizer for the details before you capture the meeting in your calendar and commit yourself. Once you have the details, make some time to prepare and be ready for the meeting.

The day of the meeting, show up on time. Nobody likes to be kept waiting. Remember, while you may not value your time just yet, others do.

The meeting organizer has all the rights to the meeting and invites the guests. You are a guest unless you called the meeting. If you called the meeting, you are the host, so you are the one to welcome the guests to speak after calling the meeting to order. In a meeting, only share the relevant information to the meeting and nothing more. If asked about something you are not sure about, feel free to say you will investigate it and get back to the host. Do not be tempted to give your own opinions unless you feel that your own opinions have been informed; otherwise, avoid thinking yours are more important than everybody else's.

The meeting agenda sets the goal for the meeting. Most meetings are for information, confirmation, or decision-making, so observe and listen and determine the reason for the meeting and act accordingly.

In addition to attending the invited meetings, you will also be involved in a variety of other meetings; some you will call, and others you will be invited. Here are a number of these types of meetings and your role:

Daily meetings with your team. These meetings are mainly for information. You are expected to inform, motivate, and inspire your team.

For your peer group and other leaders. These meetings should be collaborative in nature. The goal is to influence your peers and other leaders to either support your cause or the organization's cause.

For your boss and executives. These meetings are both informational and also to influence them to either support and/or collaborate with you and your team as you work toward the same organizational goals.

In every meeting, remember to honor other people's time and learn to listen. Meetings for me remind me why I have two ears and one mouth. So even when I call the meeting, I listen twice or more times than I speak.

Your role for the meeting lingo is that of a *master communicator.*

The tool kit for the *master communicator* starts with a working computer or a phone with a camera.

The second tool in the tool kit is a quiet place to hold the meetings.

The third tool in the tool kit is a sense of humor.

SKIP into the meetings with the Cs and avoid embarrassing yourself.

*S*equester the details of the meeting in advance.

*K*now and understand your role in the meeting.

*I*ncorporate your ideas with the agenda at hand, and do not create your own agenda.

*P*articipate fully and play full out.

The three Cs for meeting:

*C*onsider the facts and the opinions of others. You were either invited to the meeting, or you invited others to your meeting, so the opinions of others matter.

*C*ivility is not a choice but a requirement for meetings.

*C*ommitment to the meeting's cause goes a long way as most meetings do not happen once; they happen over time. So before you commit to attending, find out the number of occurrences thus far.

Action points for the meeting lingo

List down three agenda items for your next meeting.

1. _____
2. _____
3. _____

Write down three items you will use for your next meetings.

1. _____
2. _____
3. _____

Write down three clean jokes you can share.

1. _____
2. _____
3. _____

CHAPTER 11

The Dress Code Lingo

"The epitome of sophistication is the utter simplicity".

—Maya Angelou

In the health care industry, there is a dress code, especially for the staff. The dress code could be in the form of scrub uniforms or formal/casual wear. Find out from either your boss or your human resources representative what the dress code expectation is for your new role. Most organizations also have policies and procedures regarding dress codes. Look for dress code policy, as in your role, as you are not only going to be responsible for your own dress code but also for your direct reports' dress code.

Personally, I think people make the dress code more complicated than it really is. The main rule of thumb is to wear clothes that do not show too much of your skin and/or your undergarments. I know someone will be reading this and wondering if you are supposed to wear a long-sleeved turtleneck and long pants, and my answer is no. My general rule of thumb is to be conservative with your dress code when at work. For women, wearing outfits showing half of your belly, both your breasts, all your thighs, as well as your undergarments, is not acceptable. Attracting attention to your anatomy by your dress code is not the way to start your new role. Find a person who dresses well and is simple in your organization and ask them for a referral. In addition, invest some time in the nearest mall and have someone help you choose some work outfits, which are both cost-effective and modest.

Your role name as you work the dress code should be *tasteful*.

Be *tasteful* in your style. In addition, keep it simple and real. There are some unspoken rules on dress code. You do not have to wear expensive clothes to be tasteful. You can be on a budget and look well-kempt.

The tool kit for your *tasteful* self is composed of the following:

An affordable budget. You do not need to go in debt to look stylish and be presentable.

An honest shopping buddy. Yes, someone who will tell you the truth about an outfit you are about to buy.

A style magazine or catalog of your choice.

An alteration specialist who can help when you either gain or lose weight, so your clothes can be classy.

SKIP to your dress code looking fabulous with the Cs.

*S*trive for a style you are both comfortable with and meets the organization's dress code by being modest.

*K*nead your wardrobe to meet your style needs.

*I*gnore trends and fads. Have a wardrobe you can comfortably use year-round based on the weather, regardless of the current trends.

*P*arrot good looks. You can easily check for great looks by reading fashion magazines.

The three Cs:

*C*ompile a collection of affordable outfits that are beautiful and that fit your style.

*C*oordinate your colors tastefully. Nobody wants to be led by a clown, even on Halloween nights.

*C*ompliment great and beautiful looks.

Action points for the dress code lingo

List three favorite outfits from your wardrobe.

1. _____
2. _____
3. _____

Write down three of your favorite colors.

1. _____
2. _____
3. _____

Write down three names of your favorite shopping store brands.

1. _____
2. _____
3. _____

CHAPTER 12

Email/Text Message Etiquette

"Push notifications are the death of time management".

—Chet Holmes

In addition to learning the business lingo with the numbers, it is important that you learn how to communicate effectively, may it be in emails, texts, or verbally.

In today's world, we have so many ways to communicate, from text messages to virtual videos, emails, and good old-fashion verbal communication. Believe it or not, in your new role, you will begin to receive quite a lot of emails from either your direct reports, your boss, or other department leaders. Three rules that are easy to remember and follow.

Your role in email etiquette is the *savvy wizard*.

As a *savvy wizard* know your organization's security requirements regarding electronic communications and your role as a manager. Ask questions like, can you take your computer home? And if yes, what is required of you?

Now to emails, first, read the email and find out what the goal of the email is when sent. Some emails are for information only; others are for your action; while still others need your attention immediately due to the level of importance. If an email is for information only, then know the information. If action is requested, then deliver. And do so in a timely manner. If the email is marked as high importance, then attend to it firsthand. The unspoken language of business is you should always look at the email from your boss and address that email first and fast, whether your boss's email is indicated high importance or not. The fact is bosses do not send emails to find out how you are doing, but mostly, bosses send emails that require both your attention and your timely response. Over the years, I have learned that sometimes my boss may be in meeting and a question that requires my clarification is asked, so my prompt response is essential for my boss to respond with accurate information in real time.

Group emails. Group emails are tricky. But the best way to handle group emails is to remember that the only person who needs your feedback is the sender. So unless the sender indicates to reply to all, for heaven's sake, restrain from hitting the Reply All button and only reply to the sender.

Second, when communicating in emails, be objective and brief. No one likes to read a long-winded email with only two important messages repeated over and over.

Third, your responses should be brief, courteous, and to the point. Only give the required information and not your opinions and/or your feelings toward the subject matter.

Fourth, if you must complain in an email, which is not advisable to do, then do so tactfully as the recipient can decide to use the email to your disadvantage. And instead of hitting delete, decide to forward the email to either your boss or somebody else you did not intend to see the email. Remember, there is something called the email trail, and you want to make sure that your trail does not derail the email train.

Sometimes when the email is not clear, or you are not quite clear, it is helpful to give yourself and others the benefit of the doubt and pick up the phone to clarify an email message instead of muddling the emails further with back-and-forth questions and clarifications.

Text messages. By now, everyone in leadership knows about text messages, unless they live in Plato's cave somewhere, which is not true if you are reading this chapter.

You can use text messages especially if you must respond in a short monologue, mainly with yes or no. Be careful to watch for spell-check, especially if you are using a voice-over. I remember once,

I was using my smartphone voice to respond to my boss and said, "Thank you," and the voice-over kept repeating a curse. The more amused I got and started laughing, the more the words deteriorated to curse words till I gave up!

Second, keep the message short and grammatically correct. Try not to make it so hard for your recipients to where they must keep on texting back and forth, asking what your text means.

Use emojis sparingly and correctly, especially if texting your boss. I once mistakenly texted my nephew a crying emoji when I wanted to send another icon and was surprised when he asked why I was crying and if everything was all right.

To avoid a long text message or mixed messages, it's preferrable to send an email first and then text and refer your recipient to see the email.

If using a company phone, remember that the phone is company property, and everything you send through the phone and/or computer is subject to a subpoena as evidence.

Be the best savvy wizard you can be when you do the following:

SKIP to emails and the business lingo effortlessly with the three Cs.

*S*hun all language not befitting your business lingo, and have no skepticism about your learning abilities and opportunities, either formally or informally. You can do this within the organization or outside its domain.

*K*eep focused on preparing your mind to accept the new business lingo.

*I*terate the new business lingo.

*P*amper yourself with great words and knowledge that promote your change and growth.

The three Cs:

*C*oncede you do not know the business lingo initially, and be open to learning new ways.

*C*ompare and contrast your current language and/or habits to the business lingo.

*C*ompose a new business lingo vocabulary notebook for your use. Once you are confident you have nailed the business lingo down, share with your NPG and others.

Action points for emails/text messages etiquette

List three new words you learned this week.

1. _____

2. _____

3. _____

Write down three things you will stop doing to comply with email etiquette.

1. _____

2. _____

3. _____

Write down three things you commit to start doing for your email.

1. _____

2. _____

3. _____

CHAPTER 13

Managing Your Time

"Time is more valuable than Money".

—Jim Rohn

When I got promoted, I started working sixty hours a week instead of my paid forty hours a week. There is no joy in working sixty hours per week while getting paid for forty. With time, I learned how to change the trend as I did not want to get burned out to the point where I no longer loved what I did on the unit.

Word of caution: Remember the fact that you, as a manager, do not stop yourself from being an employee of your organization. Yes, you are a manager. And whether you like it not, you are still an employee of the organization, and you are paid for the value you add to your organization and not for your altruistic reasons. Just so you know, donating twenty hours of your precious time to the organization every week does not make you a hero but shows how I once, and maybe you now, may be in need of managing time at work. I would like to share with you how to manage your time more effectively.

Your new role name as you manage your time is *time superintendent*.

Your first order of business as a *time superintendent* is to find out where you are spending so much of your time. Yes, have a pen and paper ready for this analytic and write down where and how you are spending your time. After having completed the many action points thus far, this will have become second nature. The exercise should start with twenty-four hours of every day and end with zero hours at the bottom. Feel free to use the time inventory tool included for this exercise. Once you have a clear picture of how you are spending your time, you are now ready to do the following:

Figure out what you want to spend your time on. In other words, create your dream schedule by removing items you no longer wish to spend your time on moving forward.

Second, look at your dream schedule and insert the must have items and times—for instance, mandatory meetings with your boss and/or your team. Create an action plan to follow up on your matrix schedule and work the plan.

After you have found out where you are spending your hourly time, figure out how you want to now dedicate those hours and follow up with a written action plan. You will likely need to block a time, once a week, for planning your week ahead and evaluating progress toward your overall goals.

Your time is important to you and is valuable, and you owe it to yourself to protect your time with everything you've got. If you do not believe this, try to look at your employees' timecards and notice how any time, after the forty hours a week, the organization automatically calculates OT as time and a half. Every organization, at least in the USA, knows to comply with the wage laws, so why don't you do yourself a favor and work hard at demanding OT on yourself, even though you are now an *exempt* employee, and you certainly do not *qualify* for OT from your organization any longer? Yes, you are reading right, create a jar for any OT you work in any given week. And for that OT time, cut yourself a check at the end of the pay period. (Calculate the OT as time and a half.) If the practice of cutting yourself an OT check does not deter you to stop robbing yourself of some precious time, have someone else do it automatically for you before you even receive your pay, and that will surely get your attention. When I tried these two strategies, I calculated my hourly rate and learned that it was far too low. This recalculated hourly rate really got me to stop the OT habit, since most of my direct reports were almost making double what I was, even though I was a manager.

Most health care organizations, especially in the USA, advocate for some sort of work-and-life balance or work-life integration. Contact your organization's benefits coordinator, and explore how you can make use of such a benefit.

I have seen and heard way too many managers argue that money is not their motivating factor with comments like, "It's not about the money." My response to them has always been, "Yes, money has everything to do with what you are doing because you are not in the volunteers' department but on the organization's departmental payroll."

If you want to volunteer your time or be an altruistic martyr, all health care businesses have a volunteer department, and you can stop wasting your time on the organization stipend and join any other cause that is free to join.

Tell yourself the truth, and the truth is you need the money to meet financial obligations, like most, and your payroll check is an important factor as to why you are employed in the first place. If you sincerely do not need the money, then go do some charitable work, which you are passionate about, and stop collecting a paycheck.

If you are on the organization stipend every week, biweekly, or monthly, depending on how often you get your paycheck, then please hear me out and respect and defend your time like your life depended on it, as it really does.

I have spoken with quite a lot of managers who do not have a specific time when they go to sleep, and worse still, they do not have a priority of what to tackle first, even if the task that needs handling is literally staring them in the eye. Don't fall into the time trap of doing whatever comes your way, if you're tempted to do whatever comes your way, as you will be in someone else's priority list to either tackle or be tackled.

While we are on the priorities list, I would diplomatically urge every manager, to which this may apply, to stop stealing your employer's time by doing things you are not paid for while on the clock, such as completing your homework for graduate school. Seriously, your employer is paying tuition reimbursement and your rent/mortgage, and the best someone can do is steal time with the knowledge of your direct reports. Say it isn't so. Whether you get caught or not doing your homework, you are stealing time, and you need to hold yourself accountable before someone else reports this activity as it surely will be at some point. Set yourself up for success by deciding times for every activity. While at work, be at work, and do work. And when it's time to sleep, get busy sleeping at home.

I would also encourage you to plan your activities on the following themes: "I must do..." "I want to do..." "I will do..." and "it is good to do..."

1. Must do
2. Want to do
3. Will do
4. Good to do

As you notice, the first is a must-do and is extremely important and needs your attention, which means that 50 percent of all the activities you set up to do, you have no choice than to finish, leaving you enough remaining time to decide what you are going to do with the next 50 percent of your dedicated time. A great word of caution: This does not mean you bring a 50 percent mindset to the tasks at hand as no one wishes to spend time with such a coworker, a five-out-of-ten broker, so to speak. I would imagine, if you are the person reading this book, you are as close to a ten as possible. At the bare minimum, be an eight on your worst days and see how good it feels to be a nine or a ten!

SKIP to your time management genius with the three Cs.

*S*top looking for wasted or lost time after completing your time analytic. Once time is lost, you cannot find it, and the practice of repeatedly searching for wasted time only adds to your bad habit of losing time.

*K*eenly watch your time, like the American Eagle, and guard your time with a goal to maximize every second to the fullest.

*In*cise bad habits that are robbing you of your quality time, and replace the bad habits with great and creative habits by inculcating insights from self-improvement teachers mentioned previously.

*P*erpetrate to defend and guard your time with everything else you got. Prosperity is yours once you master your time as we all start with twenty-four hours each day and end with a balance of zero by the end of the day.

The three Cs.

*C*alibrate all your time tools, and align them with your goals. Maximize every effort, and have time working for yourself even when you are sleeping.

*C*ast away the time wasters in your life.

*C*auterize and reclaim the fact that you are the cicerone of your time and your life.

Some new managers have a mentality that they are very important (smile). They work long hours, eat lunch at their desk working, carry their work to the beach when they are supposed to be on a beach vacationing, etc. The truth is, you are as important as far as you are valuable to yourself, your team, and your organization. Showing up to work tired, stressed out, and out of breath does nobody any good. If you do not believe me, try missing a day of work, and see if your department would close because you are out. Worse still, God forbid, you get sick and out for a month and see if the unit would close because of your not being there. I have seen managers very frustrated after they resign or step down, and within weeks or even days, a replacement is put in place. My advice to you is to spend your time wisely, and enjoy every moment of it as this life is not a rehearsal for a better life tomorrow but the real life for you to live *now*.

Action points for time management

List three things you are spending time on.

1. _____

2. _____

3. _____

Write down three must-do items you will do.

1. _____

2. _____

3. _____

Write down three things you will do differently.

1. _____

2. _____

3. _____

CHAPTER 14

Job Requirements/Expectations

"Success has a thousand Mothers; failure is an orphan".

—Benjamin Franklin

Before I forget, I would like to fill you in on one secret regarding your job requirements or your job expectations. As a manager, there are ongoing job requirements. Once hired or promoted, your employer may set some mandatory formal or informal courses for you to attend. Formal requirements may include, but not limited to, graduate degrees, certifications, etc., while informal courses may include organizational in-services or state regulations. Be sure to find out what the requirements are as well as the deadlines.

The never-told secret is the fact that your boss expects you to lead by example. And if your supervisor has to chase you down to complete or meet requirements, there will be a looming cloud of doubt about how well you are able or can manage others if you cannot manage your time without constant reminders. Be the first to meet any deadline and encourage your teams to do the same.

Certifications can make or break your managerial career. Most professional management certifications require you to have about two years of management before one can sit for the certification. A word of advice is to start preparing for your certifications the moment you make up your mind that being a manager is what you want for your career choice.

For the certification preparations, your role is that of *certification genius*.

The certification genius tool kit.

The first tool for the certification genius is your concentration and focus.

The second tool is a good review book for the specific certification.

The third tool for the certification genius is some time, minimum of thirty minutes per week, to review preparatory certification requirements. Begin with writing down action points.

SKIP to your certification with the three Cs.

*S*earch for certifications that fit your professional goals, and match your expertise level.

*K*now your limitations.

*I*ndicate your intentions to certification early on in your managerial life.

*P*ractice and check for updates on the certifications needed.

Three Cs

*C*oncentrate, focus, and review weekly. There are free resources from most professional organizations.

*C*ontrol only what you can, and that is mainly you. There will be a lot of things that will happen in your managerial journey, and most of them, you will have no control over. The only thing you have control over is your focus. As a new manager, focus your efforts on being the best you can and capable of being.

*C*arry on even when you feel like you do not have an idea what to do next.

Action points for job requirements and certifications

Write three job requirements that are a must for your role.

1. _____

2. _____

3. _____

Write three certifications that are required for your role.

1. _____

2. _____

3. _____

State three goals you want to accomplish with your certification.

1. _____

2. _____

3. _____

FINAL WORD

I wish you well in your journey as manager beyond your first three years. As you start and continue with your journey, take some time to reflect on your leadership journey. During your reflection, think of one word that future generations would use to describe either you or your leadership style or both when you are no longer in your position and are no longer abiding in this world. Write the word down, and see whether the road you are taking as your journey is leading you to your future self. Keep in mind that the list should be fun and customized to you and your hero leaders who you admire. I did my reflection, and I would love to share with you my ongoing list:

George Washington—courage
Nelson Mandela—forgiveness
Mahatma Gandhi—patience
Mother Teresa—love
Martin Luther King Jr.—dreams
John F. Kennedy—vision
Pope John Paul II—unity
Ronald Reagan—humor
Barack Obama—change
Margaret Thatcher—decisive
Benjamin Franklin—innovation
Dr. Terry Carter—tenacity

APPENDIX A

Sample of my top reasons and my boss's top reasons:

My reasons	My boss's reasons
1. Promote teamwork in unit	employee engagement
2. Promote team integrity	improve quality metrics
3. My personal growth continues to grow	growth in leadership
4. Not work weekends	be on call every other weekend.
5. Work only four days a week (work four ten-hour shifts a week or two twelve-hour shifts and two eight hours a week)	Work five days a week for eight hours per day
6. To serve the team in any way possible	My positive energy and attitude to work with the team

APPENDIX B

Sample of the reconcilable reasons between my reasons and my boss's reasons:

Reconcilable reasons between my reasons and my boss's reasons
1. Work on employee engagement, starting with improving teamwork and organizational values.
2. Improve quality metrics.
3. Growth in leadership, both formally and through work experience.
4. Partner with other departments for weekend calls, and ensure all weekends calls are covered.
5. Work five days/eight hours a week but can flex as necessary.
6. Use my positive energy and attitude to serve and to grow with the team.

APPENDIX C

Time management inventory tool:

Where are you spending your time?

No.	Activity	Number of hours
1	Sleeping	6 hours
2	Eating	
3	Shopping spree	
4	Grocery shopping	
5	Meetings	
6	Commuting	
		Maximum total = 24 hours

APPENDIX D

Managing your time step-by-step

Step one:

1. Block at a minimum one hour a week on your calendar with this: "meeting with the most important person on earth—*me*."
2. Get comfortable.
3. Grab a drink.
4. Put on your favorite music.
5. Get ready, set, and go.

Step two:

1. Find out where you are spending your time by using the time inventory tool.
2. Mark the three things that you must do (e.g., sleeping).
3. Mark three things that you will do.
4. Mark three things that are good to do.
5. Mark three things that you want to do.

Step three

1. Block time on your calendar for the three must-do items.
2. Block time at a minimum of one hour a day for the will-do items.

3. Forget everything else and complete your calendar with the must-do and will-do items only.

Step four

1. Work your plan.
2. Have fun.

BIBLIOGRAPHY

Aldrich, Jim. *Climbing the Healthcare Management Ladder: Career Advice from the Top on How to Succeed.* Baltimore: Health Professions Press, 2013.

Borkowski, Nancy. *Organizational Behavior in Health Care.* Sudbury: James and Bartlett, 2011.

Connors, Roger and Tom Smith. *Change the Culture: The Breakthrough Strategy for Energizing Your Organization and Creating Accountability for Results: Change the Game.* New York: Penquin Group, 2011.

Cooper, Harris. *Research Synthesis and Meta-Analysis: A Step-by-Step Approach.* Washington DC: Sage Publications, 2010.

Covey, Stephen R. *Living the 7 Habits: Stories of Courage and Inspiration.* New York: Simon & Schuster, 1999.

Covey, Stephen R. *The 8th Habit: From Effectiveness to Greatness.* New York: Free Press, 2004.

Freud, Sigmund. *The Future of an Illusion.* Seattle: Norton, 1989.

Hill, Napoleon. *How to Own Your Own Mind.* New York: Random, 2017.

Johnson, Craig E. *Meeting the Ethical Challenges of Leadership: Casting Light or Shadow.* Thousand Oaks: Sage Publications, 2005.

Jung, Carl. *Man in Search of a Soul.* New York: Harvest House, 1933.

Jung, C. G. *Psychological Types.* New York: Routledge, 2017.

Maxwell, John C. *Failing Forward: Turning Mistakes into Stepping Stones for Success.* Nashville: Thomas Nelson, 2000.

Maxwell, John C. *The Complete 101 Collection: What Every Leader Needs to Know.* Nashville: Thomas Nelson, 2009.

Maxwell, John C. *Thinking for a Change: 11 Ways Highly Successful People Approach Life and Work.* New York: Warner Business Books, 2003.

Maxwell, John C. *Ultimate Leadership: Maximize Your Potential and Empower Your Team.* Nashville: Thomas Nelson, 2015.

Murphy, Joseph. *The Miracle Power of Your Mind.* New York: Penguin Random House, 2016.

Murray, Mary and Leslie Atkinson. *Understanding the Nursing Process in a Changing Care Environment.* New York: McGraw Hill, 2000.

Northouse, Peter G. *Leadership Theory and Practice.* Thousand Oaks: Sage Publications, 2007.

Peterson, Jordan B. *Maps of Meaning: The Architecture of Belief.* New York: Routledge, 1999.

Riggenbach, Jeff. *The CBT Toolbox, Second Edition.* Eau Claire: PESI Publishing, 2021.

Robbins, Tony. *Life Force. How New Breakthroughs in Precision Medicine Can Transform the Quality of Your Life.* New York: Simon & Schuster, 2022.

Robbins, Tony. *Unlimited Power: The New Science of Personal Achievement.* New York: Free Press, 1997.

Studer, Quint. *A Culture of High Performance: Achieving Higher Quality at a Lower Cost.* Gulf Breeze: Fire Starter Publishing, 2013.

Sullivan, Eleanor and Phillip J. Decker. *Effective Leadership and Management in Nursing.* Upper Saddle River: Pearson Princeton Hall, 2009.

Tyson, Paul. *Returning to Reality: Christian Platonism for Our Times.* Eugene. Lutterworth Press, 2015.

Zig, Ziglar. *A View from the Top: Moving from Success to Significance.* Shippensburg: Sound Wisdom, 2019.

ABOUT THE AUTHOR

Dr. Terry Carter is a consultant, CEO, and president of Terry International Consulting.

As a consultant with over thirty years of experience, Dr. Carter has had the opportunity to mentor hundreds of first-time managers on a quarterly basis and knows firsthand the struggles of first-time managers. Having started her career as a first-time manager, Dr. Carter knows firsthand how challenging the first three years of any manager are and intends to inspire and encourage first-time managers on their journey as they manage and lead their teams.

Terry International Consulting is based in Houston, Texas, USA.

Printed in the USA
CPSIA information can be obtained
at www.ICGtesting.com
LVHW041520140924
790863LV00003B/474